TROLLS

ALICIA Z. KLEPEIS

Cavendish
Square

New York

CREATURES OF FANTASY

TROLLS

BY

ALICIA Z. KLEPEIS

CAVENDISH SQUARE PUBLISHING · NEW YORK

Published in 2017 by Cavendish Square Publishing, LLC
243 5th Avenue, Suite 136, New York, NY 10016

Library of Congress Cataloging-in-Publication Data

Names: Klepeis, Alicia, 1971- author.
Title: Trolls / Alicia Z. Klepeis.
Description: New York : Cavendish Square Publishing, 2016. | Series:
Creatures of fantasy | Includes bibliographical references and index.
Identifiers: LCCN 2015049733 (print) | LCCN 2016008582 (ebook) | ISBN
9781502618580 (library bound) | ISBN 9781502618597 (ebook)
Subjects: LCSH: Trolls--Juvenile literature.
Classification: LCC GR555 .K53 2016 (print) | LCC GR555 (ebook) | DDC
398.21--dc23
LC record available at http://lccn.loc.gov/2015049733

Editorial Director: David McNamara
Editor: Kristen Susienka
Copy Editor: Rebecca Rohan
Art Director: Jeffrey Talbot
Designer: Joseph Macri
Production Assistant: Karol Szymczuk
Photo Research: J8 Media

CONTENTS

INTRODUCTION

Above: In John Bauer's 1916 work *Root Trolls*, a group of trolls curiously watches over a human child.

Since the first humans walked Earth, myths and legends have engaged minds and inspired imaginations. Ancient civilizations used stories to explain phenomena in the world around them, such as the weather, the tides, and natural disasters. As different cultures evolved, so too did their stories. From their traditions and observations emerged creatures with powerful abilities, mythical intrigue, and their own origins. Sometimes, different cultures encouraged various manifestations of the same creature. At other times, these creatures morphed into entirely new beings with greater powers than their predecessors.

Today, societies still celebrate the folklore of their ancestors—on-screen in TV shows and movies such as *Doctor Who, Once Upon a Time,* and *Star Wars,* and in books such as the *Harry Potter* and *Twilight* series. Some of these creatures existed, while others are merely myth.

In the Creatures of Fantasy series, we celebrate captivating stories of the past from all around the world. Each book focuses on creatures both familiar and unknown: the elusive alien, the grumpy troll, the devious demon, the graceful elf, the spellbinding wizard, and the harrowing mummy. Their various incarnations throughout history are brought to life. All have their own origins, their own legends, and their own influences on the imagination today. Each story adds a new perspective to the human experience and encourages people to revisit tales of the past in order to understand their presence in the modern age.

TROUBLESOME TROLLS

"Beneath the rock—the trolls sleep;
Amongst the trees—the trolls watch;
Under the bridge—the trolls wait;
Up the mountain—the trolls sing;
In the storm—the trolls howl.
And at the threshold of night
—the trolls come."

BRIAN AND WENDY FROUD, *TROLLS*

FROM MISCHIEVOUS MOUNTAIN DWELLERS to bridge-side bullies, trolls come in many forms. They appear in stories from cultures around the world and have **captivated** peoples' imaginations for centuries. You may have read about trolls in some of the Harry Potter books. Or perhaps you've seen trolls singing in the Disney movie *Frozen*. Whether in ancient folktales or modern-day board games, trolls are depicted in many different ways, and while these tales have been around for hundreds of years, some continue to wonder: are trolls real beings or simply a matter of imagination?

Opposite: Norwegian Theodor Kittelsen's 1906 artwork *Forest Troll* shows an oversized troll that blends in with the tree-covered landscape.

The Troll Family

Throughout troll tradition, there have been many kinds of mythical troll-like creatures. The troll "family" includes creatures ranging from forest trolls to the more human-looking "hulder people." Some folklorists say that gnomes are the smallest of the troll tribe. Over the centuries, the appearance of trolls and some of their behaviors have changed. For example, while most trolls can't stand sunlight, British author J. R. R. Tolkien created a new breed of trolls, the Olog-hai, who were able to withstand the sun's rays. Trolls have also been **purported** to be very curious and do not always treat humans with respect. Some of the more modern trolls, however, are less mischievous and kinder to humans.

Common Troll Traits

The creatures belonging to the troll family share some common features. For instance, almost all trolls are said to be ugly. These fantastical creatures are also greedy. Many like to steal from people. Some even steal the actual people themselves. Beautiful princesses are often the objects of interest for **boorish** trolls. Trolls are known to play tricks on people. Some try to swap their babies for human babies.

Another common troll trait is simplicity. Trolls are easily outwitted when interacting with people. This causes trolls much frustration and disappointment.

Storytellers and legend makers don't always feature trolls behaving in the same manner. Occasionally, trolls will help human farmers, such as by looking out for their livestock.

This huge, ugly cave troll was made out of fiberglass by artists in New Zealand.

Appearance of Trolls

Nowadays, many people get their ideas about trolls' appearances from nineteenth-century myths and folktales. Even though trolls are regularly described as ugly, their physical characteristics vary depending on the culture or the tale. Some trolls, like the fairly harmless *nisse*, are so ugly they are cute. But the trolls in Tolkien's *Lord of the Rings* series are revolting, frightful creatures.

Trolls are often gray or green in color. Sometimes, these mythical beasts have scaly skin. Most trolls have enormous noses. In some legends, trolls have used their long noses to stir pots of soup cooking over a fire. Some trolls even tuck their noses in with a belt if they're in the way.

Trolls are not known for having great vision. Some trolls have only one eye, like a Cyclops. Icelandic legends commonly feature one-eyed trolls. In folktales like "The Boys who Met the Trolls in the Hedal Woods," multiple goblins share an eye. They must rely on one another to see.

Trolls are hairy in some legends. Other tales feature smoother creatures. Some trolls in Denmark (**Scandinavian** trolls) are said

John Bauer's 1904 illustration titled *An Old Mountain Troll* has a sad and lonely feel to it.

to have either crooked backs or humps on their backs. Particularly in more modern stories, trolls have tails. However, the length of these tails can vary. Troll tails can be short and stubby like a bear's or a pig's. Others are longer, like a cow's. Trolls often tie their tails behind their backs to keep them hidden from human sight.

With respect to size, trolls throughout history have tended to be very large. This is especially true of mountain trolls. The trolls in the Lord of the Rings movies are huge. Troll features are often not proportionate. They commonly have short, stubby arms and legs and fat, sometimes droopy bellies for their body size. Troll feet are massive. The trolls in the Harry Potter films have only two toes with two giant toenails.

Female Trolls and More Unusual Troll Varieties

Smaller varieties of trolls do exist in folklore. The *tomte* of Sweden, the *nisse* of Norway and Denmark, and the *tonttu* of Finland are typically not taller than 3 feet (0.9 meters) tall.

Female trolls, also called troll **hags**, are not always depicted as ugly as their male counterparts. Norwegian female trolls are sometimes described as beautiful. They often have long, red hair. An illustration from the classic *D'Aulaires' Book of Trolls* even shows a female troll wearing golden earrings and what appears to be a sweater and skirt.

Occasionally, writers break tradition with the notion of ugly male trolls. Trolls have been described as elegant or even more handsome than their human neighbors. Some legends say that if a person sees an elegantly dressed man or woman in the forest, he should look out because it must be a troll. The well-respected Swedish ethnologist Ebbe Schön said trolls should be treated with respect because they are "the nobility of the forest."

While many trolls seem to be unclothed in folklore, some do wear clothes. The trolls in Ebleloft, Denmark, wore pointed red caps and gray jackets. Those in Gudmanstrup wore long, black clothes. Scandinavian artists Theodor

The troll depicted in Theodor Kittelsen's *Trollkjerring* has an extremely long nose.

Kittelsen and Rolf Lidberg often depicted trolls as wearing old rags, much like their poor human neighbors.

Where Trolls Live

The lands where trolls dwell are shrouded in mystery. According to some sources, trolls live in a mirror-like world. This causes these mythical creatures to see things differently from human beings. What people might perceive as dirt (or worthless), trolls might see as treasure—and vice versa.

Throughout folklore, trolls can be challenging to find regardless of where they live. They avoid daylight and often blend in with the scenery. For example, some forest trolls, such as those seen in Theodor Kittelsen's 1907 depiction, appear rather shaggy and covered with trees themselves.

Storytellers have told tales of trolls for many centuries. Most often, trolls in these tales have made mischief for humankind. They also affect the appearance of the landscape sometimes. Some people believed that giant rocks strewn about the Scandinavian landscape were the remains of trolls who exploded or turned to stone because they were exposed to sunlight. Especially in the days before scientific evidence could explain how erosion or other natural processes shaped the landscape, trolls provided a reasonable explanation for how places looked. As Norwegian folklorists Ingri and Edgar Parin d'Aulaire said, "Near by stands a cracked and weathered stone, and you don't even need imagination to see that it is one of those trolls that turned around and looked into the rising sun, which is the end of all trolls."

Denmark's Krølle Bølle

Way out in the Baltic Sea lies an island called Bornholm. This island is part of Denmark. On this beautiful, forested, mysterious island is said to live a famous troll named Krølle Bølle. This naughty troll became a picture book character back in 1946, when writer Ludvig Mahler published stories he had told his son.

Krølle Bølle's name tells about his appearance. In the Danish language, *Krølle* means "curl." This troll has both curly hair and a curl in his tail. The word *Bølle* means "thug." Like many trolls, Krølle Bølle is naughty. He also has two small horns on his head, like many of the trolls on Bornholm.

According to legend, Krølle Bølle was born on the 249-foot (76 m) high hill called Langebjerg. Some say that he lives underground. He is said to live with his mom Bobbasina, dad Bobbaraekus, and sister Krølle Borra. Local folklore says, "Every night at midnight, Langebjerg opens up and all the trolls come out." Krølle Bølle has adventures all through the night each night.

Denmark's Bornholm Island is reputed to be home to many trolls, including Krølle Bølle.

Krølle Bølle is somewhat of a celebrity in Denmark. His image can be found on goods from ice cream to jigsaw puzzles to snack bars. Some folks say that if you come across small people roughly the size of a ten-year-old wearing red hats and woolen clothes on Bornholm, they might be Krølle Bølle and his fellow trolls!

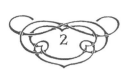

CHURCH BUILDERS AND PRINCESS KIDNAPPERS

"Long before there were people, there were trolls."

LISE LUNGE-LARSEN, *THE TROLL WITH NO HEART IN HIS BODY AND OTHER TALES OF TROLLS FROM NORWAY*

SEEKING OUT THE ORIGINS OF TROLL mythology is an adventure. Those looking for the earliest troll tales will find a winding path through the rich history of Scandinavia. Folklorists have found incredible troll stories dating back to the Viking days. Some sources say that the troll race began with a frost giant named Ymir from early Norse mythology. As author Jan Beveridge says, "Out of Ymir's feet sprouted trolls, ugly creatures with three, six, or twelve heads." Other folklorists note that Norway has had trolls ever since this time.

However, Norway is not the only place with troll legends. The mountains, caves, and forests of Scandinavia have **abounded** with tales of trolls large and small. These creatures are typically hidden

Opposite: A stone sculpture of Ymir sits amidst the greenery in Grosvenor Park, in Chester, England.

amidst the incredible landscape of Norway, Sweden, Denmark, Finland, Iceland, and beyond. Since the Dark Ages, the people living in these lands often believed that their home countries were full of trolls and other mythical creatures.

Norse Myths and More Modern Tales

Trolls trace their roots back to early Norse mythology. As Norwegian filmmaker André Øvredal said, "We've had the trolls since the Viking age, so I think it's part of our being, practically." Even the word *troll* has Scandinavian roots. The word troll appears in Old Norse and Swedish. The comparable Danish word was "trold." In medieval Norse myths existed cruel giants known as jotuns/jotner/jötunn. These mythical creatures were considered to be the main enemies of the gods. They were said to dwell in the mountains of Utgard. Much like later versions of trolls, the jotuns were huge, extremely ugly, and dim-witted.

In ancient folklore, trolls are depicted as living in deep forests, in high mountains, and sometimes by the shore. Legend has it that as the Norsemen, or Men of the North, moved into troll territory, the trolls moved deeper into the forests and mountains. Why? They did not want to be seen. Some of the early Scandinavian trolls were said to live in castles carved out of stone. Throughout folklore, the homes of trolls can be quite elaborate. They are often full of treasures collected by these greedy monsters. As expert Carol Rose comments, "They [trolls] lived in communities under the hills in long burrows and ancient earthworks. Their homes were said to be wonderful palaces of treasures that may glow at night."

From Viking times until today, Scandinavian nations have told many troll tales. A common troll myth features a troll taking a

princess away from her home. The princess's family is **distraught** by her disappearance. In some tales the king offers a fortune, something like half his kingdom, in exchange for the princess. The hero of the tale typically finds a way to outwit the troll. He gets the princess back, leading to a happily-ever-after existence for the princess and her savior. The evil troll who stole the princess often meets a bad end. Sometimes the troll is tricked into being outside when the sunlight appears, thus being turned to stone. Other tales have the hero kill the troll by chopping off its head with an enchanted sword, for example.

In *Half a Kingdom*, Ann McGovern's retelling of an Icelandic folktale, the author switches up the gender roles. In her story, female trolls capture Prince Lini, then put a spell on him using magic fog. They hold him captive and demand that he marry one of them. A poor but very clever peasant girl named Signy hears that the king is offering a reward for returning his son. Signy hides in the trolls' **lair**. She finds out that each day the trolls go outside and toss a giant golden egg back and forth between themselves. The eavesdropping Signy hears the trolls say that if they drop the egg, they will disappear forever. Signy and the Prince conspire to break the egg, turning the trolls into fog and causing them to vanish for all eternity. After claiming her prize from the king, Prince Lini asks Signy to marry him. She tells him, "We can share half the kingdom and share adventures, too, for the rest of our lives." This provides a happy ending with a more modern heroine.

In Swedish mythology, trolls are not necessarily seen as evil creatures. Instead, they may be portrayed as misunderstood beings who are naïve and rather primitive. Despite the fact that Sweden's trolls are often strong and huge, they are not too bright and can be

easily outwitted by even the youngest humans. If angered, Swedish trolls often resort to using their magical powers. This leads to people fearing the giant creatures.

Trolls' Connection to Christianity

Christianity has definitely played a role in troll mythology. Some say there is a connection between trolls living underground and the Biblical character Eve. One day while Eve was bathing her many children, God paid her a visit. Eve was not done bathing all her kids when God showed up. So she hid the children who weren't clean yet. When God inquired, "Are there not more children?" Eve told God no. In reply, God said to Eve, "Then let all that is hidden remain hidden." The children whom Eve had hidden from God became known as *De Underjordiske* ("the ones living underground").

Huldra (or Hulder) was said to be one of Eve's hidden children. Somehow she was able to remain above ground. In Scandinavian lore, she is neither seen as good nor evil. The troll-like Hulder rustles about in the woods. Ingri and Edgar Parin d'Aulaire describe her as "the beautiful Hill-maid with golden braids and a cow's tail, who walks through the forest scheming to get herself a Christian for a husband, for if she can her soul too will be **eternal**."

The perception of trolls through the ages changed over time. During the early days of Christianity in Scandinavia, some tales say that trolls helped to build Christian churches. According to a folktale called "The Handshake," Saint Olav (the **patron** saint of Norway) got a troll named Skaane to help with building the church in Seljord.

Over time, troll mythology became intermingled with the Christian beliefs and ideas. In one tale, a man called Heide

defeated a troll in a new and unusual manner: he drew a ring around the mythical beast and made the sign of the cross at him. Because of Heide's actions, the troll was fixed to that spot forever.

Ingri and Edgar Parin d'Aulaire are known for their excellent children's books and accompanying illustrations.

A number of folktales featured trolls throwing enormous boulders at churches. One Danish tale told of a troll who was so outraged by the loud ringing of the church bells that he hurled a massive boulder at a church one Sunday morning many centuries ago. The boulder, reputedly weighing 1,000 tons (907 metric tons), missed the church but still stands very close to the place of worship today. Some legends even suggested that trolls could smell the blood of Christian men. Because trolls were believed to possess magical powers, some folks associated them with the devil. Trolls became symbols of olden times, likely with more **pagan** beliefs, which were condemned by Christianity.

Trolls and the Landscape

Troll mythology is deeply connected to the actual landscape in which these mythical creatures are said to dwell. From its remote islands to its deep fjords, Scandinavia is said to be abundant with trolls. Some places, like Norway's Trollfjord, are even named after these mythical creatures. The Giant Cut (or *Jutulhogget*) in eastern Norway's Østerdal Valley is said to have been made by trolls, showing how big these creatures were.

To this day, throughout Sweden and Norway, certain rock formations are associated with the locations where various trolls

Norway's Trollfjord features steep sides and a narrow entrance, which make for some spectacular scenery.

were believed to die. For example, central Norway is home to a place called Trold-Tindterne, meaning "Peaks of the Trolls." Legend has it that the stone crags here are the remains of two troll armies that fought a great battle but that were so focused on their conflict that they failed to see the sunrise coming. The end result was that "they were changed into the small points of rock which stand up noticeably upon the crests of the mountain."

In 2012, travel writer Gail Simmons was visiting the Lofoten archipelago, off the Norwegian coast. She said of the landscape, "Clouds parted to reveal the ragged peaks of ancient, secretive mountains, and I could quite believe trolls still lurked here undiscovered. Lofoten is a landscape where nature and myth mingle." This sense of nature and mythology intermingling has been an essential element of troll folklore through the centuries.

Particularly since the nineteenth century, folklorists around the world have written down troll tales. These stories have featured trolls of all varieties—from the craftiest cave trolls to ones that help on the farm. Adults and children from ancient Norsemen to modern-day mythology buffs have been captivated by rich troll stories. And this fascination is likely to continue for years to come.

Trolls With Many Heads

One of the strangest varieties of trolls is the troll with many heads. Such terrifying creatures appeared even in early Norse mythology. Writer J.B. Eriksen said, "Initially the trolls had six heads and six arms and quickly grew to a monstrous size. Ever since that time, Norway has been inhabited by these giants."

Ingri and Edgar Parin d'Aulaire feature a number of multiheaded trolls in their classic *d'Aulaires' Book of Trolls*. According to them, "The more heads a troll had, the wilder and more fearsome he was." So a troll with twelve heads would be twelve times stronger and fiercer than a troll with only one head. What happened if a twelve-headed troll got angry and roared? He would get twelve nasty headaches.

Theodor Kittelsen's 1905 painting *Mountain Troll* features a troll with many heads.

The d'Aulaires told a tale about a twelve-headed troll who was searching for a king with twelve daughters. Why? So each head of the troll could have his own maiden. Once the troll found such a king, he threatened to destroy the kingdom if the king did not hand over his beloved daughters. The king was too frightened to refuse. The daughters were taken away to the troll's distant mountain home. A brave young man, fortified by liquid from the troll's magic flask, was able to wield the troll's huge sword. "The lad swung the sword so well that all the heads flew off at once." He helped the princesses to escape, returning home with lots of silver and gold from the troll's lair. The lad's reward was half the king's kingdom and marriage to the youngest and prettiest daughter—a classic ending to a troll tale.

KNITTERS, SHAPESHIFTERS, AND CHANGELINGS

"Trolls vary greatly in size. While the biggest troll may be as large as a mountain some are hardly above human size and can live comfortably under bridges or in barns."

GEORGESS MCHARGUE, *THE IMPOSSIBLE PEOPLE: A HISTORY NATURAL AND UNNATURAL OF BEINGS TERRIBLE AND WONDERFUL*

FROM THE DAYS OF THE EARLIEST myths told round the fire, trolls have possessed special powers. Since these creatures are fantastical, it makes sense that their legendary talents are dramatic and wide-ranging. Trolls are said to be great at feats of strength, building things, and even shapeshifting.

Storytellers from around the globe have celebrated trolls' incredible physical strength. From throwing gigantic boulders to waging battles, trolls are able to wreak havoc with both human and goblin enemies. According to writer Georgess McHargue, "Mountain Trolls are naturally the biggest of the family. They are reputed to have the strength of fifty men ... "

Opposite: A boy runs away from an enormous troll in Theodor Kittelsen's 1905 oil painting *The Ash Lad and the Troll*.

Because trolls are not particularly clever, humans have sometimes been known to use the trolls' brute force to their advantage. In a retelling of a classic Norwegian folktale called "The Eating Competition," a young boy called Ashlad fools a forest troll into believing he is physically stronger than the troll. Ashlad has a bag of homemade cheese. He squeezes the bag hard, making it drip. Ashlad tells the troll that he has just squeezed white rock. He says that if the troll doesn't obey him, he will squeeze the troll in the same way. The foolish troll is scared. He says to the boy, "'Nay, my dear fellow, spare me! I had no idea you were so strong. I'll help you chop,' he whimpered." The troll quickly chopped many cords of wood for Ashlad.

Builders, Knitters, and Healers

Trolls are also reputed to be excellent builders. They make things out of metal and stone. In Norse mythology, some trolls live in castles carved out of stone.

Troll women are said to enjoy knitting. According to authors Brian and Wendy Froud, "They find it so enjoyable that they can often be seen knitting a ball of roots into clothing, creating garments of complicated designs and patterns."

Some folklore describes trolls as gifted healers. They are reputed to use magic, herbs, and other items found in nature when concocting their healing mixtures. But these mythical beasts have not always used their magical powers for healing. Sometimes they would inflict illnesses on people. According to the Troll Blog website, the trolls were capable of "shooting magical projectiles that randomly hit people. They had particular[ly] great influence on children."

Shapeshifting: Amazing Troll Trickery

An essential part of troll mythology is these creatures' ability to shapeshift, or change themselves from one form to another. Most of the time trolls choose to remain hidden from people's view. However, shapeshifting is an incredible asset to creatures that desire to remain hidden from or sneak up on humans.

In some stories, a troll might change itself into a log or a stub. But if a person took out a knife and tried to cut that log, the troll would run away. Why? Trolls can't stand steel. Perhaps trolls hate steel because it is not a natural substance.

Trolls also change themselves into the forms of different animals, such as snakes, dogs, or cats. In a retelling of an old German folktale, author Fritz Eichenberg tells of a troll named Ruebezahl. This gigantic troll, wanting to spy on a pretty girl, "changed himself into a black raven and flew to the top of a tall ash tree overlooking the pool, to enjoy this lovely spectacle." The troll then decided to change again, this time into a handsome young man. Storytellers have celebrated trolls' supernatural ability to shapeshift for many centuries.

A cloaked figure of Rüebezahl almost blends in with the wooded background in Austrian artist Moritz von Schwind's painting.

Trolls As Changelings

Throughout folklore, troll children are described as monstrous. They behave badly and are ill tempered. In fact, sometimes when human children are naughty, their parents will refer to them as troll-like. Norwegian author Lise Lunge-Larsen says that when she was behaving badly as a young girl, her mother would call her *en trollunge*, meaning "troll child."

John Bauer's 1913 painting *The Changeling* shows trolls with the changeling whom they have raised.

Troll babies are known to cry and wail all day, much to the dismay of their mothers. Occasionally when these troll mothers cannot take it anymore, they have a sneaky solution to their predicament. They take a better-behaved human baby from its crib and replace him or her with their own dreadful troll offspring. This monster child is known as a changeling.

In the Shetland Islands, located off the north coast of Scotland, there are legends of trolls known as trows. These trows are sometimes switched for human babies because trow babies were thought to be sickly and weak. Unfortunately, if a human baby failed to develop properly or was different in some ways from its "normal" siblings, people sometimes explained the abnormalities by saying their baby had been switched with a trow baby.

British author Thomas Keightley told a story about a changeling in his 1850 book *The Fairy Mythology*. According to the tale, a trow left a changeling at a farmhouse. The human baby was taken by the trows into the hills. One night a tailor who'd been working at the farmhouse woke to the sound of music. When he looked, he found the changeling dancing amidst a whole group of fairies. The tailor watched for a while but then blessed himself. According to the tale, "On hearing this, the trows all fled in the utmost disorder, but one of them, a woman, was so incensed at this interruption of their **revels**, that as she went out she touched the big toe of the tailor, and he lost the power of ever after moving it."

In some changeling tales, the human parents will head to the hills in search of their babies. Swedish author Selma Lagerlöf wrote a famous story simply titled "The Changeling." In this tale, a human woman discovers that she has a troll changeling living with her. She asks others how to get rid of it. They advise her to beat or mistreat the troll baby. However, the woman cannot bring herself to do that. Her husband even throws the changeling into their farm that is burning. But the woman rushes to save the troll child. Her husband leaves her on account of the changeling. He meets his own son in the woods. He also meets the mother of the changeling who has shown up to exchange the human child for her own troll child. The troll mother says to the man, "I treated your child better than you treated mine."

In this 1895 illustration, a man named Silverwhite fights a giant green sea troll.

The Sjötroll of Finland

Water-dwelling trolls are among the most mysterious in Scandinavian mythology. Finland has an evil lake-dwelling troll called the Sjötroll. According to legend, this gigantic mythical creature lived on the lakebed of Lake Opp. It was confined to the depths of the water by two **runic** stones located at each end of the lake.

For many years, this enormous troll was kept deep underwater. But one day a dense, highly unusual fog appeared. This fog made the runes powerless. As a result, the Sjötroll was able to rise to the lake's surface. The Sjötroll had the chance once again to wreak havoc on the fishermen who tried to catch fish in the lake.

Some people say that a man named Gabriel Olai Hannodius was on the scene in 1680 to report the event of the Sjötroll returning to Lake Opp's surface. According to some sources, people still get nervous whenever the fog is thick enough to mask the stones' magic powers over the troll. On such days, superstitious folks don't fish on the lake. They worry that the Sjötroll will reach out and drown them beneath its waters. Whether they are right or not, we may never know …

THREE BILLY GOATS

"He was fairly average, as far as trolls go. He was big, and ugly, and hairy, with eyes as round as saucers and teeth as sharp as knives."

JOANNE ASALA, "THE THREE BILLY GOATS GRUFF"

ASK JUST ABOUT ANYBODY ON THE planet to name a story involving trolls and the likely answer would be "The Three Billy Goats Gruff." The folklorist team of Peter Christen Asbjørnsen and Jørgen Moe recorded this famous troll tale in the nineteenth century. This Scandinavian myth has been celebrated and retold by storytellers, artists, playwrights, and other creative people around the globe.

The Basic Tale

"The Three Billy Goats Gruff" is a fairly simple story. It features a troll living under a bridge, one of the classic places where trolls are believed to dwell. Probably the most commonly cited version of the tale is the

Opposite: This 1908 watercolor shows a classic scene from "The Three Billy Goats Gruff."

one from Norway. In this version, there are three goat brothers named Ole Gruff, Olaf Gruff, and Jakkob Gruff. It is springtime. The goat brothers are looking to climb up to the meadows in the mountains. There, the grass is abundant, and they can fatten themselves up.

Unfortunately for the Billy Goats Gruff, the journey to the mountainous meadows is not easy. To get to their destination, the goats need to voyage through deep forests and also cross a roaring river. But an obstacle lies in their way: a huge, unsightly, unpleasant troll. The goats know that trolls are dangerous. They wonder how they should proceed to cross the bridge. They decide to attempt the bridge crossing one brother at a time. The idea behind the single crossing is that perhaps the foolish troll won't notice a single goat passing over the bridge.

So Jakkob Gruff, the youngest and smallest of the brothers, ventures across the bridge first. His hooves clip and clop as he steps across the bridge's wooden slats. The hungry troll roars from beneath the bridge. He demands to know who is passing. Jakkob replies that he is the youngest and smallest of the Gruff brothers. He says, "I'm so small, and there is hardly any meat on my bones. Why don't you wait to gobble up my brother instead? He is ever so much bigger than I."

Being a creature of little wit, the troll sends the youngest goat on his way. He dreams of a better food source to come. Feeling emboldened by his little brother's success, medium-sized Olaf Gruff attempts to cross. His hooves make even more noise as he clip-clops over the bridge. Again, the greedy troll threatens to gobble up the second goat for his supper. Using his younger brother's strategy, Olaf suggests that the troll let him pass up to the high meadows and wait for the biggest (and tastiest) brother to come by.

Finally, the biggest and boldest brother, Ole Gruff, makes his way across the very hungry troll's bridge. He is full of swagger. He dances his way along. He shows no fear of the bridge troll. Ole, the troll who is making such a racket, announces himself. The troll tells Ole that he should wait for the troll to get a pinch of salt before he comes up to eat him. Ole Gruff tells the nasty bridge troll, "Do your worst! I've got two spears, and I'll poke your eyes right out of your head!" True to his word, the troll comes up to the top of the bridge. Ole Gruff pokes out the troll's two eyes before head-butting the troll off the bridge into the river below. The troll never bothers anyone again. The three Billy Goats Gruff make it to the high mountain meadows. They eat grass all summer and fatten themselves to their hearts' content.

Story Setting and Scandinavian Geography

"The Three Billy Goats Gruff" takes place in the mountains of Norway. The geography of this Scandinavian location can be glimpsed in a number of details strewn throughout the myth. A rushing river, crossed by a wooden bridge, is essential to the events of the story. The tale also features other elements common throughout Scandinavian troll mythology. The scenery includes deep, dense forests. Rich grassy alpine meadows, good for livestock grazing, are also featured in the story's mountainous setting.

Troll Characteristics in the Story

Many classic characteristics of trolls are sprinkled throughout this iconic myth. Much like earlier troll tales, "The Three Billy Goats Gruff" features a troll that is easily outwitted by others. He is big

and dim-witted and very **gullible**. In this case, instead of being outsmarted by human beings, the bridge troll is tricked by a trio of animals. Thinking he will get an even better meal (a larger goat, in this case), the troll awaits the next Gruff brother.

"The Three Billy Goats Gruff" also depicts a troll living under a bridge, which is a typical portrayal of these beasts. The troll also resides near the mountains, as is seen throughout Scandinavian mythology.

Some common physical characteristics of trolls are highlighted in the story. For example, the troll is large and hairy. He has big, round eyes that are compared to **pewter** plates. His nose is described as being as big as a rake handle. His knife-sharp teeth are something to be feared.

The troll here has his eyes poked out and is thrown off a bridge, both rather violent acts. And yet "The Three Billy Goats Gruff" has more of a traditional fairy-tale kind of ending. The three goat brothers seem to live "happily ever after" as they feast in Norway's alpine meadows. Many troll myths continue to have happy endings even to this day. The troll is not actually killed at the end of "The Three Billy Goats Gruff," unlike some troll myths. But after Ole Gruff battles with him, the troll doesn't go on to harm other creatures or people.

Influence of the Tale on Others

"The Three Billy Goats Gruff" has influenced writers, artists, and musicians alike for generations. Peter Christen Asbjørnsen and Jørgen Moe wrote the oral tale down in their home country of Norway back in the 1840s. They went on to include it in their famous anthology titled *Norwegian Folk Tales*. Sir George Webbe

Dasent, a professor at King's College in London, England, selected this story for his famous collection of tales titled *Select Popular Tales from the Norse*, published in 1863. Some scholars say that Dasent chose "The Three Billy Goats Gruff" for this book because, unlike some other troll myths, this one did not contain material that might upset a child of the Victorian era. This book was wildly successful. Writer John Lindow said that Dasent's books "represent a bridge over which trolls walked from Norway to Britain and thence to the rest of the English-speaking world."

Artists around the globe have been inspired to create images of trolls based on "The Three Billy Goats Gruff." In an image by artist Otto Sinding, the troll "is essentially a very large man, with shaggy hair that joins with his full beard and moustache to cover the face." Peering up from under the bridge where he dwells, artists sometimes portray the troll as being surrounded by rocks and a fallen log. This helps the troll blend in with its surroundings, as is common throughout mythology.

Artist Otto Sinding.

The British Library in London had an exhibition in 2015 titled Animal Tales, featuring a number of illustrations related to "The Three Billy Goats Gruff." Perhaps such an exhibition proves the point that modern audiences still are captivated by this simple, old folktale. A quick Google search of "BBC and The Three Billy Goats Gruff" offers kids and adults alike the opportunity to listen to an oral retelling of the tale, to view an animated version, and even to learn

This black-and-white engraving of "The Three Billy Goats Gruff" comes from George W. Dasent's book *Tales From The Norse*.

songs and rhymes related to the Norwegian troll myth, among other options.

Musicians over the last two centuries have also created works inspired by the story. These come in many forms, including brilliant operatic works geared for the youngest audiences—thus introducing children to both the troll myth itself and the form of opera. The music of well-known composers such as Mozart, Donizetti, and Rossini have helped bring "The Three Billy Goats Gruff" to life on stage. Many opera companies around the United States, such as the Piedmont Opera, have done productions of this tale.

Even modern-day Norwegian filmmaker André Øvredal took inspiration from "The Three Billy Goats Gruff" in his 2010 movie *Trollhunter*. His movie features a troll living under a bridge. It also features billy goats on the bridge that lure the troll up to where they are located.

As expert and scholar John Lindow said in his book *Trolls*, "Perhaps the most famous troll is the one under the bridge in 'The Three Billy Goats Gruff'."

Iceland's Christmas Trolls (Yule Lads)

The Christmas season in Iceland is an interesting mix of traditional folklore and religious practices. Just like in many other countries, folks in Iceland celebrate Christmas by exchanging gifts and enjoying good food. But most other nations have a single Santa Claus or Father Christmas figure. Children in Iceland are lucky enough to be visited by trolls known as the thirteen Yule Lads.

Even the youngest kids in Iceland know the story of Grýla, a frightful ogress who is part troll and part animal. She is also the mother of the thirteen Yule Lads. Grýla lives in the mountains with her sons, her third husband, and a black cat. Every Christmas, Grýla and the Yule Lads descend from the mountains. She searches for misbehaving children to boil in her cauldron. Her sons seek out mischief. Grýla can capture naughty children. However, according to legend, she must release those who **repent**.

These two Icelandic Yule Lads appear very much like Santa Claus.

In the thirteen days leading up to Christmas, Icelandic children put a shoe in their bedroom windows. Each night, one of the Yule Lads pays them a visit. Depending on how the child has behaved on the previous day, the troll might leave a small gift, a sweet, or rotting potatoes. Each Yule Lad behaves in a distinctive way. For example, Huröaskellir likes to slam doors during the night, while Pottaslelkir likes to steal leftovers from pots. One thing's for sure—kids in Iceland had better watch how they behave throughout the Christmas season … or else!

BARGAINERS, THIEVES, AND PEOPLE EATERS

"Trolls, admittedly, do on occasion like to snack upon a knight or less often a damsel and least often of all, a child, but ... the one thing trolls very, very, rarely do indeed is eat other trolls."

<small>BRIAN AND WENDY FROUD, *TROLLS*</small>

EVER SINCE TROLL TALES HAVE BEEN recounted around the fire, people have largely had a fearful feeling about these mythical creatures. For the most part, trolls are said to be living out of sight in the forests and mountainous areas. However, that does not mean that trolls and humans have never interacted. This mingling has come in different forms, depending on when and where the troll myths are told. The way that people react to trolls depends on the storyteller's perspective on these creatures. Folklore can portray trolls as mischievous, **malicious**, or occasionally even helpful beings.

Opposite: The title of John Bauer's 1915 illustration, *Good evening, old man! the boy greeted*, describes this scene perfectly.

Beastly Bargainers

In many legends, trolls are said to bargain with humans. The humans have to outwit the trolls in such tales or else suffer unfortunate consequences. One example of this type of bargaining story featured a man named Esbern. Esbern was in love with a girl, but the young lady's father would not allow his daughter to get married until Esbern constructed a fine church. A troll made a bargain with Esbern. He told him that he would build the church for Esbern. However, as is often the case in such tales, there was a catch. If Esbern could not discover the troll's name by the time the church was built, the troll would take both Esbern's eyes and his soul. Even though he tried hard, Esbern was not able to learn the name of the troll. He lost hope . . . until his beloved girl prayed for him. At that very moment (when his love prayed), Esbern heard the troll's wife singing to her baby. The song she sang contained the name of her husband. So Esbern was spared a terrible fate.

The tale of Esbern shows trolls as beastly bargainers. There were often violent outcomes for people who could not meet their end of a deal with a troll. But this story also reflects how many myths featured prayer as a weapon against trolls. This was particularly true in the times after people in northern Europe converted to Christianity.

Tremendous Thieves

From Scandinavia to the British Isles, legends abound with trolls and their thieving ways. Depending on the legend, they might steal women, children, or property (especially food). In many troll myths, the trolls seek out lovely young girls or women.

Humans are tempted by troll treasure in Erik Theodor Werenskiold's painting.

The Faroe Islands lie in the North Atlantic Ocean between Iceland and the Shetland Islands. These islands, which belong to Denmark, are home to trolls called Fodden Skemaend ("the Hollow Men"). These **dastardly** trolls were known for kidnapping people and keeping them in their lairs as slaves for many years. Some tales depict the human females combing the hair of the trolls.

Trolls are known for their love of all things shiny and valuable. This love drives them to seek out treasure. Whether living in caves or underground homes, trolls were known to possess great quantities of silver, gold, and gemstones. Sometimes a snake or a bull might even be employed to guard the trolls' treasure.

Trolls have also been known to steal food or beer from people. This was especially a danger during the holiday season. Why? During the holidays, trolls knew that people were preparing all kinds of special foods and in great quantities. So it was considered wise to be extra careful since trolls could easily sneak into human homes and eat all their food. Sometimes these nasty trolls even kicked people out of their own residences while they stuffed themselves silly. Tales such as Jan Brett's *The Christmas Trolls* or Jeanette Winter's *The Christmas Visitors* feature the holiday gluttony of Scandinavian trolls. The trolls in *The Christmas Visitors* both toast and threaten the host (Halvor), whose food they gobble down:

> A feast, a feast, a feast is nice
> With Halvor shivering on the ice.
> And he will have a curse to fear
> If he won't welcome us each year.

People Eaters and Cannibals

A common theme throughout troll mythology is that these creatures like to feast on human flesh. Whether mountain, forest, bridge, or sea trolls, they all seem to enjoy devouring people. This comes up in many of Tolkien's books, such as his *Lord of the Rings* series. Tolkien's works contain a huge variety of trolls: the Hill-trolls, the Mountain-trolls, the Cave-trolls, the Stone-trolls, and even the Snow-trolls. Expert Carol Rose describes these mythical creatures as "evil **cannibals** that descended on the village people of each region and slaughtered them like cattle for the table."

Norwegian composer Edvard Grieg crafted a piece of orchestral music titled "In the Hall of the Mountain King." Grieg wrote the music for a scene in the famous 1867 play *Peer Gynt*, written by Henrik Ibsen. The story depicts a man named Peer Gynt's adventures in the underground Kingdom of the Trolls. You can almost hear the trolls hunting Peer down, faster and faster. Peer barely gets away from the trolls—just before becoming their next meal!

In some legends, trolls are described as cannibals, meaning that they feed on other trolls. For instance, the trolls in Tolkien's books are described as "black-blooded giant cannibals."

WOOL SPINNERS AND OTHERWISE HELPFUL TROLLS

It should be noted that trolls are not always evil or malicious in folklore. There are stories in which trolls will help human beings. Carol Rose says that trolls will sometimes "endow a family they like with riches and good fortune."

According to some legends, trolls and humans had regular, everyday interactions. Especially during tough times, people and trolls might borrow food, money, or tools from each other. It was sometimes said that if a person loaned a troll some flour for baking bread, the troll would possibly return an even better quality of flour to him or her. Some troll tales also show the creatures helping farmers with their work. In particular, troll women were known for their skill at spinning wool. But humans have to be careful. Legend has it that if people give a troll something belonging to them personally, that would give the troll power over them.

Above: A troll wonders how old he is in this 1911 painting by Theodor Kittelsen.

WARDING OFF TROLLS

Humans living near trolls have always sought out ways to protect themselves from the vicious creatures. One common remedy was mistletoe. Sometimes parents placed mistletoe in their children's cradles. This was seen as a way to protect them from being stolen by trolls and replaced by changelings. Not only people could be protected from trolls by mistletoe. Swedish farmers might hang mistletoe both in a cow's crib or a horse's stall to protect their livestock against evil trolls.

Religious articles were often used to ward off trolls. Why? In later troll myths, these creatures were sometimes seen as enemies of Christianity. According to legend, some people carved crosses into the doors of their homes as a way to prevent trolls from coming inside. Religious articles were believed to protect humans against trolls. Trolls were also known to hate noise, so the sound of church bells was said to drive them away.

Trolls were thought to be afraid of things made of steel, such as scissors. Some say this was because of the steel itself. Others have speculated that it is because a pair of scissors can be manipulated to look like a cross.

In case of a troll plague, some folks suggested using salt for protection, since salt was believed to have stronger magical powers than the trolls' powers. In days gone by, salt was used to preserve foods. This probably seemed magical in the days before refrigeration.

INUIT TROLL MYTHS

"Out and about one may meet with trolls that have long claws.
These claws are sharp as knives."
Neil Christopher, *The Hidden: A Compendium of*
Arctic Giants, Dwarves, Gnomes, Trolls, Faeries, and other
Strange Beings from Inuit Oral History

MANY TROLL TALES TAKE PLACE IN Scandinavia, but troll folklore can also be found in a variety of other locations around the globe—from New Zealand to Japan to the United Kingdom. Troll mythology is especially rich in the Inuit culture. The Inuit people live in the area from northwestern Canada to western Greenland. They have a wide variety of fascinating troll tales.

Inuit Troll Lore

For thousands of years, the Inuit people have inhabited huge areas in the northern part of the planet. Today this territory makes up parts of Canada, including Nunavut, the Northwest Territories,

Opposite: This figurine, made of wood, bone, and ivory, is called a tupilak *and is designed to bring harm to someone.*

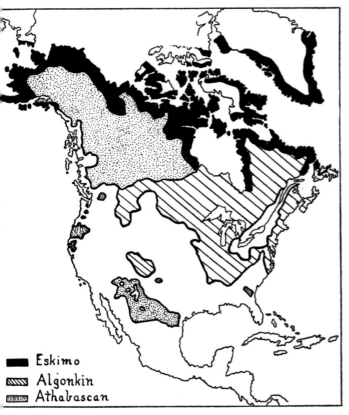

Eskimo
Algonkin
Athabascan

This 1911 language map shows where North American Inuit (called Eskimo here), Algonquin, and Athabascan are spoken/used.

Yukon, Quebec, and Labrador. Some of the harshest, most demanding environments on Earth are here. Some Inuit people believe in what is known as animism. According to this belief system, all living and nonliving things have a spirit. Traditionally, the Inuit regarded animals, rocks, food, and even sleep as being alive.

Storytelling and oral history continue to be important parts of the Inuit culture. Tales have been passed down over the centuries. These stories often deal with powerful spirits. The Inuit people believe these spirits still inhabit both the sea and the land. According to Greenland ethnographer Knud Rasmussen, monster stories (including troll tales) are just one type of legend popular among the Native people here. A number of such legends were collected during the twentieth century. Many were put into a 1972 book called *Tales from the Igloo*.

The trolls that appear in Inuit folklore are similar to the more ancient varieties of Scandinavian trolls. Throughout the folklore of what is now Canada and Greenland, the trolls are seen as **malignant**. As author Neil Christopher says, "Inuit oral history tell us of evil deeds committed long ago that transformed the souls of animals and humans into vengeful spirits … we are told that these **malevolent** spirits still roam the desolate landscapes."

As far as appearance goes, Inuit trolls are often scary and ugly. The evil creatures are both giant and hairy. They often have huge, hairless bellies that drag on the ground as the trolls move. These trolls also have razor-sharp talons at the end of their fingers. The nasty trolls of this region are said to live in the hills. There they wait for the chance to prey on humans and rip the flesh from their bodies.

The Qalupalik and Kukilialuit: Two Arctic Trolls

In some Inuit lore, troll stories are used as a way to get children to behave—or not behave—in certain ways. For example, some Inuit parents and elders tell a story about Qalupalik as a way to prevent children from wandering too close to the shore. Get too close, and they could be swept away into the icy ocean. Qalupalik is a human-like creature. She has green skin, long hair, and quite long fingernails. She lives in the sea, much like some Scandinavian sea trolls. She hums as a way to bring children closer to the water's edge. Qalupalik is said to wear an *amautik*. (This is a parka commonly worn by Inuit women.) An amautik has a pouch just below the parka's hood. This pouch holds a small child against the wearer's back.

According to Inuit legend, if youngsters get too close to the sea's edge or are disobedient, "the Qalupalik will come onshore, put them in her amautik and take them back to the sea with her to raise them as her own children, never to see their family again." So, if you ever happen to be standing along the Arctic Ocean's shore and hear humming, you'd better run fast!

There are many names for the different varieties of Inuit trolls. One such variety is a race of beings known as the *kukilialuit*, which literally means "those with the great claws." References to these beings can be found in Greenland and throughout the Canadian Arctic. According to legend, the kukilialuit live in snow huts during the winter, much like the Inuit people themselves. But these nasty

creatures eat humans, using their fierce long claws to tear at the flesh of their victims. As writer Neil Christopher notes, "It is said that the hunger of the kukilialuit is such that once they attack a person they will not cease to scratch and tear at the body until all the flesh is gone."

Kidnappers and Competitors

According to authors Denise Carmody and T.L. Brink, the traditional Inuit earth was home to goblin people. This group of mythical creatures included trolls as well as dwarfs, giants, and more. These fantastical beings "could either help travelers or carry them off to torture." Throughout Inuit mythology is the idea that trolls and similar creatures take humans away from their families and homes, never to be seen again. Cultures around the globe have similar stories of trolls kidnapping people, much to the dismay of their loved ones.

Amidst the Inuit folklore and artistry, one can find examples of the competition between humans and trolls for the limited resources that are available in the far north. After all, the Inuit live in an area where access to food is not always easy. Marine animals are a vital staple of the Inuit diet.

Artist Bruce Brenneise created a fantastic illustration titled *Troll's Bait*. It depicts a troll using a human being as bait to catch its dinner from the depths of the frigid Arctic seawater. The consequences can surely be deadly for humans who run into trolls in Inuit territory.

We may never know whether trolls still roam the harsh landscape where the Inuit people live. However, as Neil Christopher says, "although these hidden beings might now be rare, many . . . can still be found by those who venture into the remotest places of the North."

The Amajuqsuk

Throughout troll mythology are creatures that seem to possess characteristics of trolls as well as of other mythical creatures. An example of such a creature is an *amajuqsuk*. Sometimes she is described as an ogress. Others refer to her as a "troll woman." Stories about amajuqsuk have been recorded in the Netsilik Region, located on the Arctic coast of Canada. This region is home to Inuit people, including the Netsilingmiut.

An amajuqsuk is believed to be a big, powerful female creature. She is wicked. She possesses a less-than-delicate appetite (for humans). She is said to wear "a basket made of bones, antlers, and driftwood." She puts the people she has captured into this basket. Some sources say that she fills her basket with rotting seaweed, which is smelly. The basket can become overrun by big insects.

Among the amajuqsuk's captives tend to be children stolen away when adults were not paying attention. Inuit mothers use the threat of amajuqsuk to frighten their children into behaving and doing what they are told.

When researchers spoke with Inuit people in 1999, there were some differences of opinions about whether the amajuqsuks existed. One man from the community of Naujaat said that these beings no longer existed. But another from Kangiqsujuaq "reported that he saw one close to the community. He described it as a big woman wearing a big caribou amauti." Some Inuit people believe that they should not run away from this spirit. Otherwise, the result would be "death or great sickness."

"TRUST ME – YOU'VE NEVER SEEN **ANYTHING** LIKE THIS BEFORE"

DAVID EDWARDS, DAILY MIRROR

"**ENORMOUSLY** ENTERTAINING"

VARIETY

"**ASTONISHING, EXHILARATING** AND **UNIQUE**"

ROBBIE COLLIN, NEWS OF THE WORLD

"**SPECTACULAR**"

AIN'T IT COOL NEWS

TROLL HUNTER

15 TBC

JOHN M. JACOBSEN PRESENTS A FILM BY ANDRÉ OVREDAL OTTO JESPERSEN 'TROLLHUNTER'
DIRECTOR OF PHOTOGRAPHY HALLVARD BRAEIN, F.T.F. EDITED BY PER ERIK ERIKSEN VFX SUPERVISOR ØYSTEIN LARSEN
PRODUCTION DESIGN MARTIN GANT SOUND DESIGN BAARD HAUGAN INGEBRETSEN LINE PRODUCER TROND GAUTE LOCKERTSEN
POST PRODUCER MARCUS B. BRODERSEN PRODUCED BY JOHN M. JACOBSEN AND SVEINUNG GOLIMO DIRECTED AND WRITTEN BY ANDRÉ OVRE
A FILMKAMERATENE AS PRODUCTION IN COOPERATION WITH FILMFONDET FUZZ AND SF NORGE AS
WITH SUPPORT FROM THE NORWEGIAN FILM INSTITUTE AND SOGN AND FJORDANE FYLKESKOMMUNE

DOLBY DIGITAL   www.facebook.com/trollhunterUK   momentum PICTURES

FROM BOARD GAMES TO MOCKUMENTARIES

"Trolls are everywhere today. Everyone knows what a troll is, even if our personal notions of trolls might differ."

JOHN LINDOW, *TROLLS: AN UNNATURAL HISTORY*

PEOPLE HAVE BEEN TELLING TROLL stories since the Viking days. Some might say that troll mythology really hit its high point in the nineteenth century. This was the time when folklorists like Asbjørnsen and Moe brought some classic Scandinavian troll tales into the spotlight. These stories then became available to people around the world. Stories, plays, poems, and music featuring trolls were popular during the nineteenth century, particularly in Europe. Some writers used troll tales to explain unusual features on the landscape. Others used trolls' dastardly deeds as a way to frighten people into behaving well. As writer Rebecca Winther-Sørensen said of these legends, "They were often meant to scare children,

Opposite: An advertising poster for the 2010 film *Trollhunter*.

but even today they are essential and important to the modern northern society."

Of course, not everybody saw merit in folktales. Many educated people in Europe hold such myths in low esteem. Even Norway's own famous writer Ludvig Holberg believed that fairy tales were only suitable for the nursery. He went so far as to say that such tales were "without merit and ought to be banned." Luckily for lovers of troll tales, some scholars believed that this rich mythology was important to society.

Jack Prelutsky was the first children's poet laureate in the United States.

TROLLS IN THE MODERN DAY

You might wonder whether anyone still believes in trolls in the twentieth and twenty-first centuries. Writer Neil Christopher says things on the matter: "It seems that for much of the developed world, their magical inhabitants are remembered in folktales and children's stories ... But, at present, this hidden world is still part of the landscape and living memory of the North. These beings haven't yet faded into legend or myth." As the years have progressed, storytellers, playwrights, filmmakers, and musicians alike continue to keep troll mythology alive. Some folks from Scandinavia to northern Canada still believe in these mythical creatures.

A number of modern-day stories featuring trolls follow in the iconic traditions of Scandinavia. For example, the trolls in J.K. Rowling's Harry Potter books are not too clever. As Fred Weasley joked in *Harry Potter and the Goblet of Fire*, "Anyone can speak Troll. All you have to do is point and grunt." Also, just like the earlier troll lore, Rowling's trolls were huge, reaching a height of around twelve feet tall and weighing as much as a ton. They were known for being very aggressive, violent, and unpredictable.

Do all modern trolls look and act exactly like those from the Viking days? Of course not. Many modern-day writers and artists have put their own spins on how trolls appear and behave. But that's part of the fun. For example, American poet Jack Prelutsky tells of a tiny troll named Underfoot in his 1996 book titled *Monday's Troll*:

> I'm Underfoot, the least of trolls,
> No bigger than a bug,
> I socialize with mice and moles,
> My neighbor is a slug …

Prelutsky's poem takes liberty with the typical size of a troll, making it even tinier than a gnome. Instead of savagely eating a whole person, Underfoot nibbles on the toes of its victims and tickles them beneath their clothes.

Many old troll tales feature trolls making soup and having hearty appetites. But the bridge trolls in Julie Larios' poem "Trolls" make a strange concoction for supper:

Troll arms will grab you
and put you in a pot—
in with the turnips
and the dung and the spuds,
in with the beetles
and thistles from the ditch ...
You'll be a troll's supper
under the bridge.

The creators of the popular 2013 Disney movie *Frozen* also took liberty with the image of trolls as evil. Most trolls in this film, from the troll king Pabbie to the youngest trolls, seem to have a kind, loving side, and are family oriented. They even play the role of matchmaker and sing a lot.

Troll Games and Dolls

Besides movies and literature, trolls have also thrived in modern culture within the world of games. One very popular game featuring trolls is Dungeons & Dragons (D&D). The trolls in this complicated role-playing game live in the cold mountains and have fierce claws, as in traditional folklore. They are ferocious and nasty attackers. These trolls have a yellowish-green complexion and long, thin arms. Unlike in traditional tales, the Dungeons & Dragons trolls are known for their powers of regeneration. They can grow back a limb lost in battle. Another current game featuring trolls is Cave Troll. Each player in this strategy game is in charge of a party of explorers seeking to raid the cave troll's lair, searching for gold and other magical artifacts.

A quirky pop culture representation of trolls can be found in the form of dolls. These dolls got their start back in 1959 when a Danish woodworker named Thomas Dam made one as a gift for his daughter. He started selling them locally and by the 1960s, the troll doll craze was in full swing. These trolls are less terrifying than those depicted in movies and literature. They typically have big eyes, happy smiling expressions, and crazy, fuzzy hair (in a wide variety of colors). There's even a Troll Museum in New York City where visitors can see a huge collection of these dolls and other artwork featuring these mythical creatures. A movie based on the troll dolls is scheduled to be released in theaters in November 2016.

Troll dolls like this were very popular in the 1960s and 1970s.

Scandinavian Trolls Today

Curiosity about, and even some belief in, the supernatural remains strong in Scandinavia—and not just among folktale-loving children. The independent news source called *Science Nordic* published an article in 2012 titled "Why are gnomes and trolls suddenly back in the limelight?" And the Danish Council for Independent Research announced in 2014 that it would fund a PhD project that examines "the supposed presence of supernatural beings on the island of Bornholm." The recipient of the funding, Lars Christian Kofoed Rømer, plans to look into "the relationship between popular folklore and 'actual relationships' with what he refers to as 'underearthlings' that are rumored to live on Bornholm."

The people of Bornholm have really embraced the myth of troll inhabitants sharing their island home. The tourist industry thrives here, in no small part because of the belief that trolls actually do live underground on the island and come out at night. Perhaps Rømer himself shares this belief in trolls. He noted, "I think it is fascinating that the legend of the island's trolls continues to thrive in today's world and I want to look at the creatures' physical **manifestations** on the island and the way they are interacting with locals," he said.

A number of websites have reported peoples' claims to have seen or interacted with trolls. The Norwegian filmmaker André Øvredal made a "mockumentary" (what amounts to a fake documentary) called *Trollhunter* in 2010. This film features both mountain and forest trolls. Some folks have even claimed that the movie is supposedly edited from anonymous footage, though that is very debatable.

To this very day, people ask themselves the following questions: Do people really still believe that trolls exist? Are we absolutely sure that they don't? Maybe Birgit Hertzberg Johnsen, the Director of the Norwegian Folklore Archives, had it right in her open-ended way of thinking:

> Legends seem plausible and tell about events which could have taken place. Research shows that some people believe in them while others are skeptical. Legends exist in a borderland between fact and faith, or fantasy ... Are legends based on real events? We can't answer this ... [Legends] are group fantasies which fill the gaps in peoples' knowledge.

Glossary

abound To be present in great quantities.

boorish Rude or ill-mannered.

cannibal A person or an animal that eats its own kind.

captivated Attracted or held the interest of someone.

dastardly Wicked or evil.

distraught Disturbed with painful feelings or doubt.

eternal Lasting forever.

gullible Easily cheated or deceived

hag An evil or ugly old woman.

lair The resting place or den of a wild animal.

malevolent Spiteful; showing ill will.

malicious Doing mean or cruel things just for fun.

malignant Evil in influence or likely to lead to death.

manifestation A display or evidence of something.

pagan A person who holds religious beliefs that are outside of the world's main religions.

patron A person chosen as a special supporter or guardian.

pewter A metallic substance containing lead that was used in the past for utensils.

purport To appear to be or claim to be something, especially falsely.

repent To express regret for one's wrongdoing.

revels A merry or noisy celebration.

runic Relating to marks or letters of mysterious or magical significance.

Scandinavia A cultural region made up of Norway, Sweden, and Denmark and sometimes also of Finland, Iceland, and the Faroe Islands.

To Learn More About Trolls

Books

Christopher, Neil. *The Hidden: A Compendium of Arctic Giants, Dwarves, Gnomes, Trolls, Faeries, and other Strange Beings from Inuit Oral History*. Toronto, Canada: Inhabit Media Inc., 2014.

d'Aulaire, Ingri, and Edgar Parin d'Aulaire. *D'Aulaires' Book of Trolls*. New York: The New York Review Children's Collection, 2006.

Peebles, Alice. *Giants and Trolls*. Minneapolis, MN: Hungry Tomato, 2015.

Stewart, Gail B. *Trolls*. San Diego, CA: ReferencePoint Press, Inc., 2012.

Website

National Museum of Iceland

www.thjodminjasafn.is/english

The National Museum of Iceland website features a cartoon version of an ancient Viking myth.

Video

Qalupalik, **a short film by Ame Papatsie.**

www.nfb.ca/film/nunavut_animation_lab_qalupalik

Watch this short film about Qalupalik, the Inuit sea monster.

Bibliography

Asala, Joanne. *Norwegian Troll Tales*. Iowa City, IA: Penfield Books, 2005.

Asbjørnsen, Peter Christen, and Jørgen Moe. *Norwegian Folk Tales*. New York: Pantheon Books, 1960.

Christopher, Neil. *The Hidden: A Compendium of Arctic Giants, Dwarves, Gnomes, Trolls, Faeries, and other Strange Beings from Inuit Oral History*. Toronto, Canada: Inhabit Media Inc., 2014.

d'Aulaire, Ingri, and Edgar Parin. *D'Aulaires' Book of Trolls*. New York: The New York Review Children's Collection, 1972.

Froud, Brian and Wendy. *Trolls*. New York: Abrams, 2012.

Lindow, John. *Trolls: An Unnatural History*. London: Reaktion Books Ltd, 2014.

Lunge-Larsen, Lise. *The Troll With No Heart In His Body and Other Tales of Trolls from Norway*. Boston, MA: Houghton Mifflin Company, 1999.

Rose, Carol. *Giants, Monsters & Dragons: An Encyclopedia of Folklore, Legend, And Myth*. New York: W.W. Norton & Company, 2001.

"The Yule Lads." National Museum of Iceland website. Retrieved November 22, 2015. http://www.thjodminjasafn.is/english/for-visitors/christmas/the-yule-lads.

"Trolls' appearance and behavior." Troll Blog website. Retrieved November 10, 2015. http://users.skynet.be/fa023784/trollmoon/TrollBlog/files/b954ac6e9e7c2f-9e29c99a0615387157-25.html.

Index

Page numbers in **boldface** are illustrations. Entries in **boldface** are glossary terms.

ABOUT THE AUTHOR

Alicia Z. Klepeis loves to research fun and out-of-the-ordinary topics that make nonfiction exciting for readers. Klepeis began her career at the National Geographic Society. She is the author of several kids' books. Her nonfiction titles include *The World's Strangest Foods, Understanding Saudi Arabia Today, Bizarre Things We've Called Medicine,* and *Vampires: The Truth Behind History's Creepiest Bloodsuckers.* Her fictional titles include *Francisco's Kites; From Pizza to Pisa;* and *Cairo, Camels, and Chaos.* Klepeis is currently working on several projects involving world cultures and strange animals. She lives with her family in Upstate New York.